KATE ROSEWOOD

My ~~story~~
& me

Cover Artist: Joseph Adam - josephadamart.com; @josephadamart
Cover Design: Kate Rosewood
Art & Collage Design: Kate Rosewood
Collage Illustrations: Canva Pro & Shutterstock via *Everett Collection*
Revisions: Skarlet Figueroa
Editor: Dianne Kemp

ISBN: 979-8-9910330-1-5

About the title, My ~~story~~ & me

"My ~~story~~ & me," is a collection of poetry written over the course of different seasons of my life. The poetry within these pages is not solely mine—it is also yours. The "_story_" is crossed out to signify how our words and meanings can be interchangeable in our lives & between different people. Many poems contain blanks, inviting you to insert a word, emotion, or action that represents your individual journey.

The most beautiful aspect of the human experience is sharing these moments together, _never alone._

About the cover art

The stunning cover painting for "My ~~story~~ & me," titled _"Sunlit Tantra," & "Elysian,"_ adorning its front and back covers is a vibrant masterpiece by Joseph Adam, created in collaboration with me, Kate Rosewood. This captivating artwork captures the essence of a fun frolic on a summer day, with playful swirls and splashes of color representing the mischievous charm & radiant beauty of the season. Inspired by joyful summer moments & the visual narrative of emotional release, Joseph Adam's painting adds a visual celebration of summer's exuberance, perfectly complementing the uninhibited expression of emotion in my poetic journey throughout the book. Discover more of his work at josephadamart.com.

About the art design

The art design is intentionally crafted to enhance and deepen the symbolic meaning of the poems through lyrical expression. The black & white imagery represents the inner world of life's difficult experiences, with the black pages reflecting emotional suppression. As you progress through the poetry book, color gradually fills the pages, symbolizing the hope that connects us to authentic & raw emotions. This transformation serves as a powerful metaphor for overcoming emotional repression, embarking on a liberating journey toward vulnerability, acceptance, & healing.

This
is my
therapy for life:
to be
authentic, bold,
vulnerable, & brave.
to hold all the pieces
of what makes us
human,
look back
smile & say,
"it was tough,
but let's do it all again
anyway."

Thank you from the bottom of my heart for picking up My ~~story~~ & me. Each poem is a piece of my journey, a fragment of my soul, & I am honored to share it with you.

I hope these words resonate with you, offering comfort, understanding, & healing.

With all my love,

Kate Rosewood xoxo

For anyone
who needs to be
seen,
heard,
& validated.

your story is <u>yours.</u>
you are enough.

Theme Song

Iris - The Goo Goo Dolls

My *mind*
& me

Words are never enough;
I need you to feel what I feel,
see what I see,
know what I know

then,
just maybe,
you'll finally understand
me.

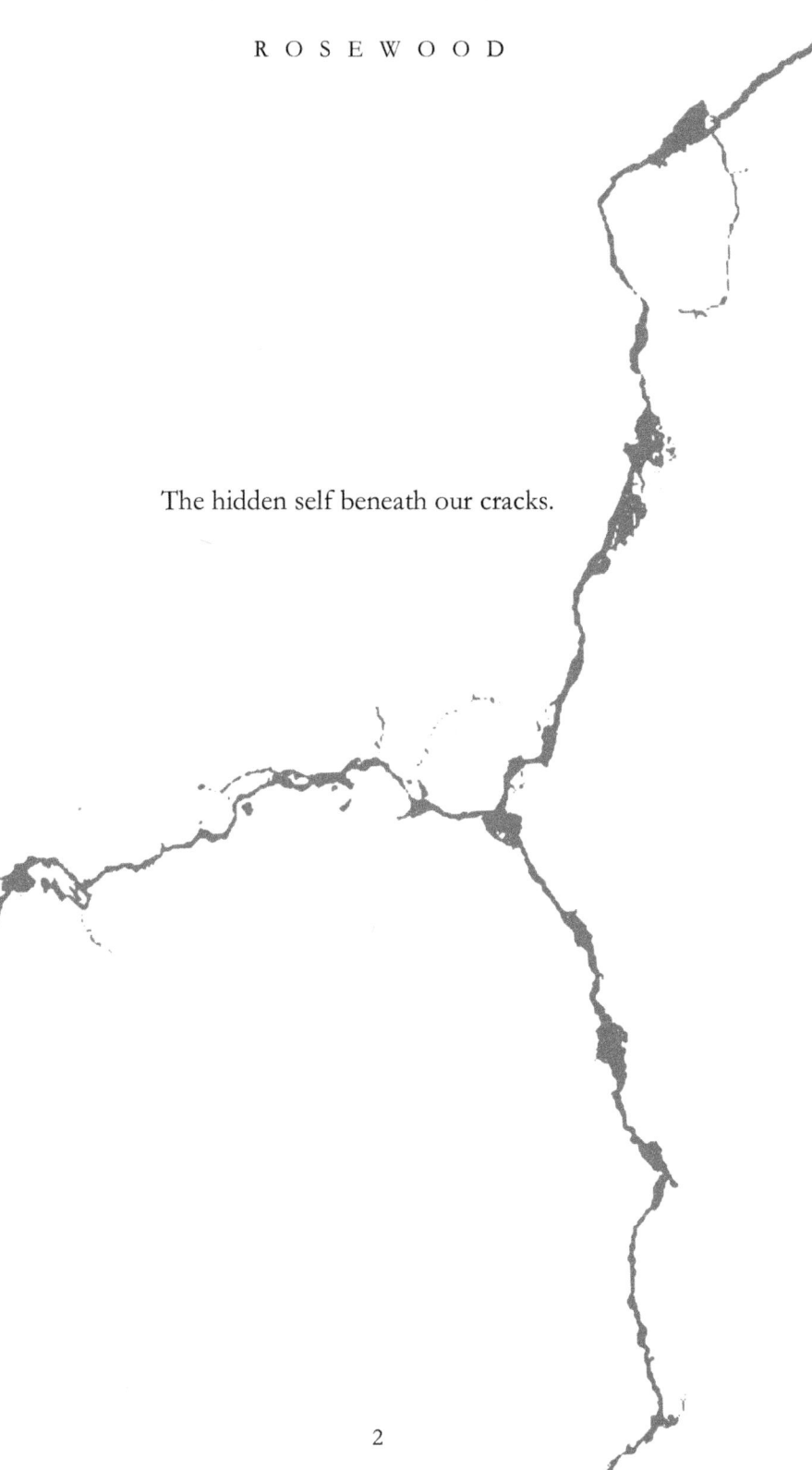

The hidden self beneath our cracks.

My desire
is to win
wars
against my feelings
of ~~inadequacy~~ _____.

I am a
mess of
beauty
in the
brokenness.

Why are you like this?
who did this to you?

me, myself, & I.

~~Anxiety~~ _____,
my constant companion:
an uninvited
guest
at the table
of my life.

You're unpredictable,
unavoidable,
& impossible to ignore—
my unseen force,
shadowing every step,
ever-present & inescapable.

you have overstayed your welcome.

Each breath
paints the world
in shades of static.

a struggle against the weight of existence.

You show me my flaws,
aiming for a fix,
a relentless pursuit,
unveiling,
all that *I'm not.*
my self-worth
ripped at the seams,
lost in the shouts
of expectations
of who I
should be.

Control,
a false illusion
of
freedom.

My *story* & me

I build walls only I can *see*,
but everyone else can *feel*.

I hold onto yesterday's worries,
unaware it's tomorrow's burden.

I am the architect of my own ruins.

What if my worries
are just rehearsals for tragedies
that *never* happen?

~~Peace~~ _____,
a game of
hide & seek.

Confrontation
the action to unspoken truths—
a threshold I hesitate to cross,
an uncertainty of
safety or silence,
awaiting me,
demanding courage,
but all I feel is

d
   r
     e
       a
         d.

I'll try again tomorrow,
maybe.

not.

Each time a person exits my life,
it affirms everything I have feared.
I am unloveable.

I just need to be *enough*.

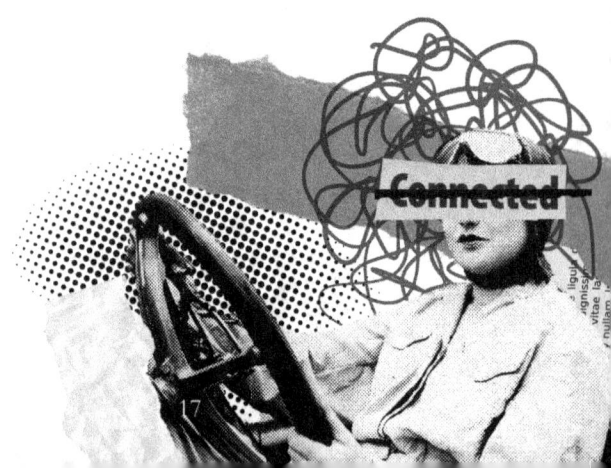

~~Fear~~ _____,
the driving force
behind *every*
thought,
choice,
decision.

a blueprint of my regrets.

I catastrophize
to know the ending,
but always end up
with plot twists.

I hate
when
my thoughts,
that are lies,
become
actionable truths.

my mirage.

My ___*story*___ & me

~~*Self-sabotage*~~ _____,
manifesting your worries
& wallowing in the consequences.

Impulse reigns;
fixations start.
thoughts collide
chaos, my art.

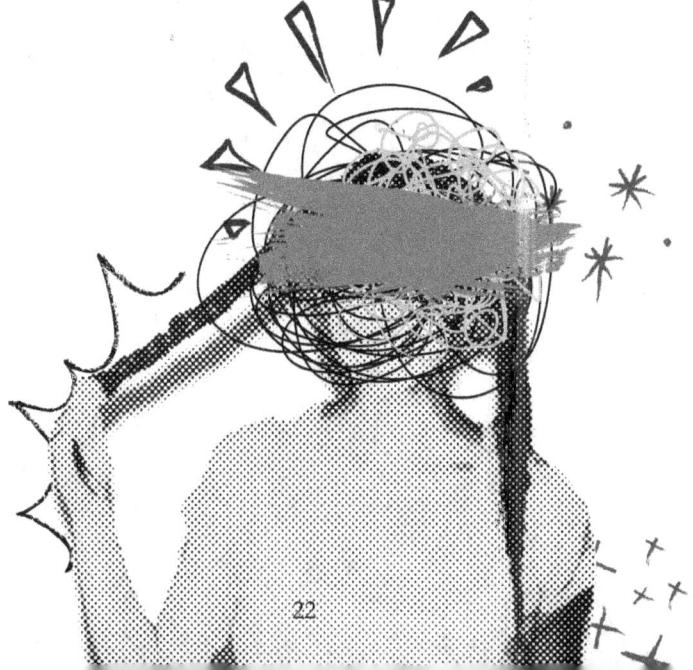

I hate you.
I love you,
sometimes.

the curse of having an overactive mind.

I always look for answers
where there is no solution,
to remind myself
my own problems are
small in comparison.

My ~~story~~ & me

Sometimes,
knowing
is worse than
not knowing.

the gift of ignorance.

I cannot accept myself;
I need more,
I want more,
constant whispers of "*not enough*"
plague my soul,
hoping that the words of affirmation
fill the void.
I know,
deep down,
only *I* can fill.

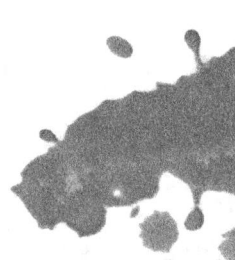

30 seconds to make an impression;
a lifetime to keep it.

no pressure.

I am a girl whose identity was stolen,
constantly in search of a new one.

I was
the girl
who always said
"yes"
& was too
afraid
to say
"no".

~~People pleasing~~ _____,
is a
disease
that destroys
everything
that made me,
me.

I was the clay you molded.

People
who can't be
themselves
are like puppets
attached to strings,
being controlled
by every living thing.

I am the project of control & manipulation.

I don't recognize *you* anymore
I miss you.
I miss us.
I miss the way *we* were.
searching for myself,
who got lost in yesterday.

come back to me.

I've lost
my own
reflection.

I am
the mirror image
of what you
created me
to be.

an ever-changing shapeshifter.

My voice
echoed loud,
not just in
words,
but in the
quiet
spaces between.

I was the actor
for everyone's script
for my life.

"I guess," I said.
"I know," I thought.

You always told me
what was *wrong,*
while I lost myself,
trying to hear from you
what was *right.*

In my thoughts,
I rehearse
your lines,
countless times,
perfecting them,
in hopes
to believe
they are *mine.*

My _story_ & me

Chasing smiles,
forgetting *mine*.

My shadow follows me,
a painful reminder
of everything,
we *used* to be.

They used you,
like a piece of clothing:
bought you,
wore you,
adored you.
then,
the style of you
was out,
& they,
returned you.

all sales not final.
worn out, but never chosen.

An endless cycle,
offering myself
entirely,
expecting nothing
in return.

My _story_ & me

You dismiss what I ~~feel~~ _____,
when my emotions are _real_.

It's the *weight*
of every unspoken word,
the *ache*
of every unshed tear,
it's the *silent* scream
within my soul;

it's not just *emotions*,
it's the breaking of my *spirit*.

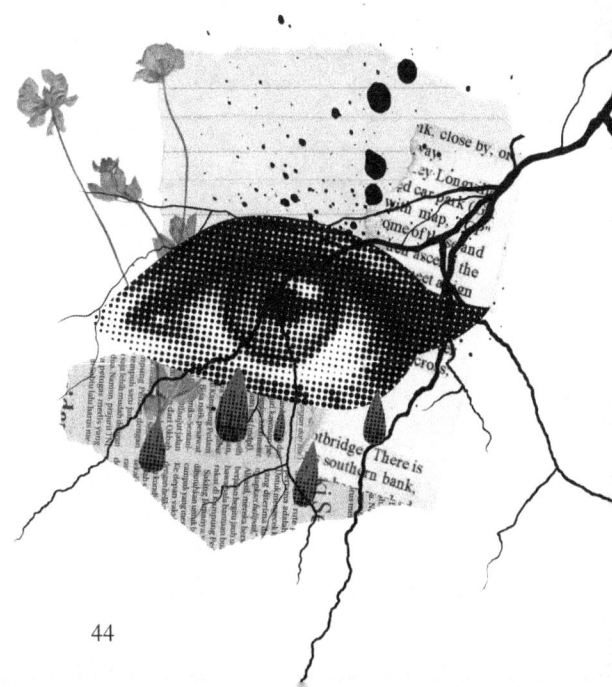

What's the point of fighting battles,
I am pre-destined to lose?

fates defeat.

I don't want to be selfish,
but *selfishly*, I do.

~~Resentment~~ _____,
the heavy
shadow,
behind every
fake smile.

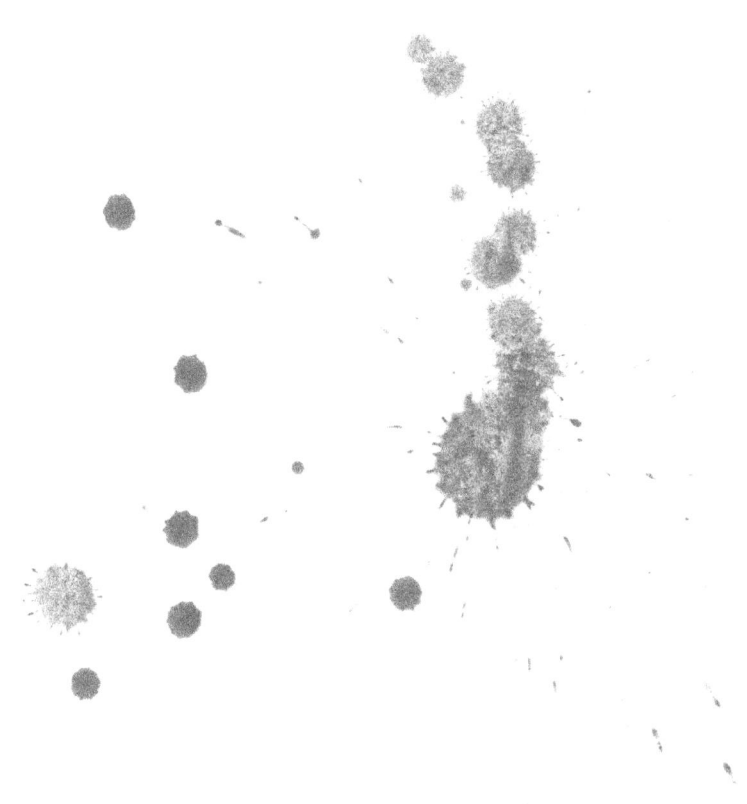

The only thing
that made me
fall
were the people
who made *me*
jump.

my individuality drowned in the applause of the crowd.

"It's fine," I said.
"It's not," I thought.

Is ~~avoidance~~_____ going to be a reoccurring event in my life?

To be invited,
is all I wanted,
even in my
absence.

I look for
answers
in children's books,
like roadmaps,
seeking lessons
in life
instead of
living it.

the reader versus the author.

~~Perfection~~ _____,
a relentless duel of
who I am
versus
who I am not.

My intuition cries
when I embrace
deceit.

I know what
I want
is what
I can't have.
then,
why do I
still strive,
to have it?

the paradox of unrealistic expectations.

~~Comparison~~ _____,
kills,
steals,
&
lies,
the person
I *knew,*
the person
I *was.*

Nothing
is more
discouraging
than
reaching for
a part of
yourself
that was never
there.

I'm chasing
a memory
that never
existed.

Repeat.
same
choices,
decisions,
mistakes.
repeat.

my cycle.

I want to change,
but struggle to change.
it's easier to stay in
hell
than to climb out of it.

a prisoner to myself.

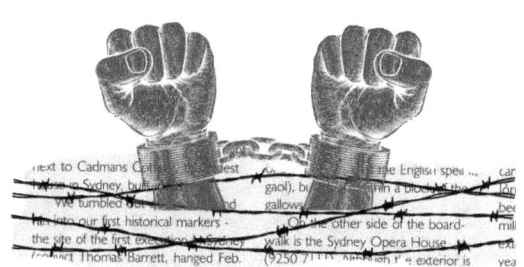

My ~~burdens~~ _____,
unseen chains,
a silent fight
without a name,
battling the unknowns
of suffering & pain.

I let my demon out of my cage
when life gets boring;
it likes to play.

destruction battles peace.

62

My _story_ & me

In following shadows,
I found my darkness.

~~Lost~~ _____,
hope
without a
compass.

My ~~story~~ & me

Tearing myself apart to reconstruct a disaster.

The venom of
shame,
guilt,
blame,
animosity,
is *me*.

"Leave me alone," I said.
"Please stay," I thought.

I've mastered the art of smiling so convincingly,
even my tears believe *I'm fine.*

My ___*story*___ & me

Hope _____,
is a curious thing.
it can either bring life or death,
but nothing in-between.

My scars
hold my choices
& remind the world
of my
mistakes.

to be vulnerable.

My ___*story*___ & me

Nothing destroys the soul more than being a
~~disappointment~~ _____.

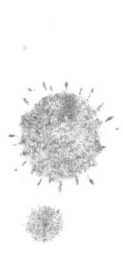

I never needed to be *fixed.*
I just needed to be *heard.*

My _*story*_ & me

~~Shame~~ _____,
the demon
I carry
on my back,
running
to escape its
grip.

Sometimes,
you just have to
smile
& pretend
everything is ok,
hold back
the tears,
&
walk away.

~~Suppression~~ _____,
turns off my
needs,
wants,
voice,
identity,

self.

the weapon that scars me.

It's hard to be in my skin,
when I am reminded by the world
why it's not enough.

beauty now a burden, disguised as a standard.

My ___story___ & me

My ~~insecurities~~ _____,
reflect
the parts of myself
needing growth & acceptance.

easier said than done.

ROSEWOOD

one
person,
to break my
confidence.

years,
to get it back.

When what you judged
is what you became
to be.

karma served to me.

For once in my life
I want to be self-serving
& give in
to everything
I desire.

damn the consequences.

I fucked up
& now
we're different.

my mind & me.

Saddest truth,
no one
will ever love me
the way I need to
love myself.

the nemesis of true love.

My _*story*_ & me

I feel
compelled
to help you
rediscover
the beautiful parts
of living.

me to myself.

I don't know
who I am
or
what I want,
but
I know
what I don't.

it ends here.

My *past*
& me

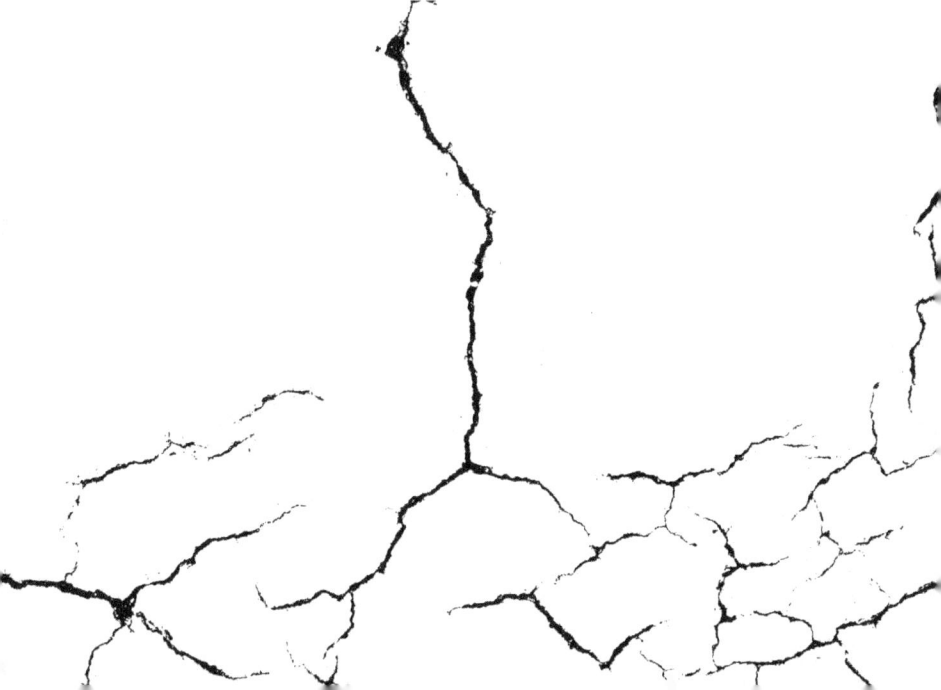

You were everything
I purposefully
avoided.

I knew I was
unequivocally & irrevocably
screwed.

The universe
held its
breath
for
you & I.

My ___*story*___ & me

No bounds,
no rationality,
no limits.

The risks & fate of falling in love.

I always
followed
the rules,
until *you*
made *me*
break them.

the rebel I became.

We were fools to consequence.

I followed you
to where all
the wild things are,
untamed spirits
searching for
a place to belong.

My _story_ & me

I looked for freedom in you, but only found chains.

There was no
past or future,
only the present,
consumed
by our desire & need
for one another.

My ___*story*___ & me

I became a vessel for your greed & pleasure.

You
explored me
like a map,
searching
for gold.

x marks my heart.

I breathed in
your exhale
with
my inhale.

a suffocating embrace.

I got
lost
in your
kisses
while you
uncovered
all of
me.

I surrendered my soul only to be exploited in your game.

Every action,
a whispered warning,
I *ignored*.

The stars
held our
truths,
our love,
unraveled them.

time tainted by deceit.

I was the
moon
bringing
balance
to your
light & darkness.

I lost my own gravity.

You
entered my life.

I
let you stay.

We were crimson,
with shades of pain,
tainted by scars
too deep to explain.
stained as maroon,
where memories seep,
ruined together
into a love
too deep to keep.

My ___*story*___ & me

Yesterday, your *world*.
today, your *problem*.
tomorrow, your *regret*.

Sometimes the brightest moments
veil the deepest shades of ~~loneliness~~ _____.

I danced with the devil,
consumed in flames,
the ashes of my innocence.

You were sin.
temptation
with no
~~redemption~~ _____.

Designed

I was your doll,
to dress & display,
searching for ~~worth~~ _____
by what others would say.

He was different from everyone else.

the lies I told myself.

I let you have all of me,
to have an inch of your heart.

I gave,
you took;
the servant
& the thief.

My <u>*story*</u> & me

I live in the empty spaces you'll never fill.

I clinged to a pain,
I mistook for passion.

Put on your mask,
you said.
hide your flaws,
you said.
smile,
you said.
be enough,
you said.

"pretend,"
I said.

striving endlessly to meet your standards.

It took one
conversation
to rewrite my
perception of
you.

Your yes
was *no.*
your sorrys
were *blame.*
your promise
was *lies.*
your love
was *hate.*

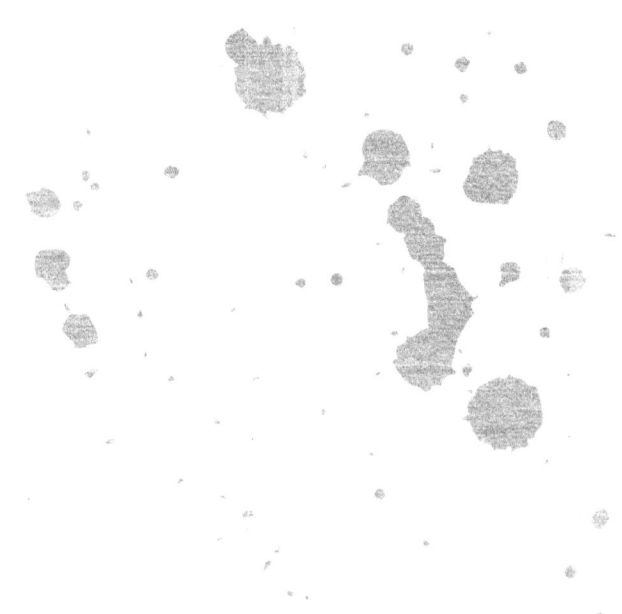

You say
"I'll change,"
but all I see
is the
"same."

I've had this
conversation
with you
a million times,
but never out loud—
only in my mind.

"I can't," you said.
"You won't," I thought.

Unfulfilled promises
are empty words,
a bottomless pit,
forever branding
you
unreliable.

Sharing my feelings with you is self-inflicted punishment.

my heart learned to stay silent.

You
were the
poison
I continued to
drink,
thinking
you
were the
antidote.

Yelling.
all noise
with no
words.

I hear you, but don't see you.

My __*story*__ & me

I would.
I should.
I could.

I didn't.

missed opportunities, wasted on you.

I apologized
for crimes my heart
never committed.

My ___*story*___ & me

I tried
to fix me,
to fix you,
to fix us.

~~I tried.~~

I failed.

Why do I
feel like the failure
for your
choices and mistakes?

I blame myself
for the
version of you
I created.

We were pawns,
sacrificing each other's hearts
for the illusion of victory.

You want space—
I lose.
you want danger—
I lose.
you want substances—
I lose.
you want money—
I lose.
you want more & more—
I lose.
lose.
lose.
lose.

you.

I'm not sure
which is worse:
being isolated
in a house
by myself,
or
feeling alone
with you
in it.

Your silence
made your
actions
loud.

Ok.
ok.
ok.

k.

We blurred the lines
between passion & possession,
believing it was devotion.

My *story* & me

We
were an
hourglass
waiting for
the last grain
of sand to

f
   a
     l
       l

Every time
you pushed
me away,
was a
test
to see if
I would
~~stay~~ _____.

I waited for you.

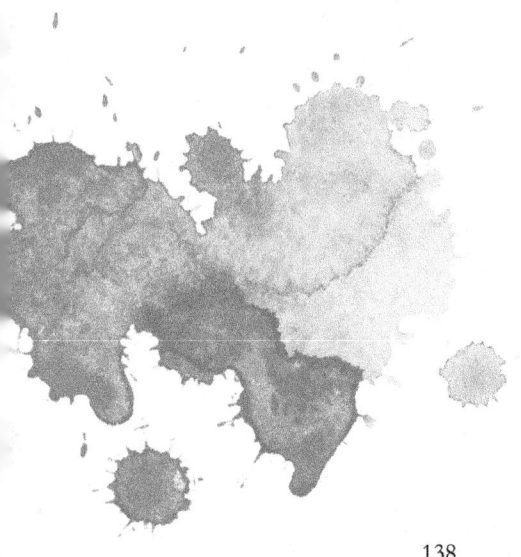

I waited for answers with no replies.

Seeds of ~~distrust~~ _____,
planted,
nurtured by your hands,
spread & rooted
in my veins,
infecting
the flourished
crevices of my
heart.

I withered away.

You said,
"there are attractive women everywhere,
but your heart is worth more than
a thousand beautiful faces."

Your fingers told the truth
when they were no longer
interlaced & knotted
with mine.

you lied.

My ___*story*___ & me

I was
another name
to add
&
~~cross~~ off
your list.

Mine.
mine.
mine.
mine.

hers.

Cast aside
no longer
claimed
~~yours~~ _____.

I was a *placeholder* _____,
for someone else.

You promised
to ~~never~~
break a
promise.
you promised
& you ~~still~~
left.

My tears
spill ~~desperation~~ _____,
smears of ~~fear~~ _____,
drowned in ~~helplessness~~ _____.

you aren't here.

My soaked pillows
serve as
a constant reminder
of the
countless hours
spent
convincing you
to *stay.*

I'd rather die
loving you,
then live
hating you.

The fact that I settled is the real tragedy.

I'm drained,
mending wounds
never meant
for my stitches.

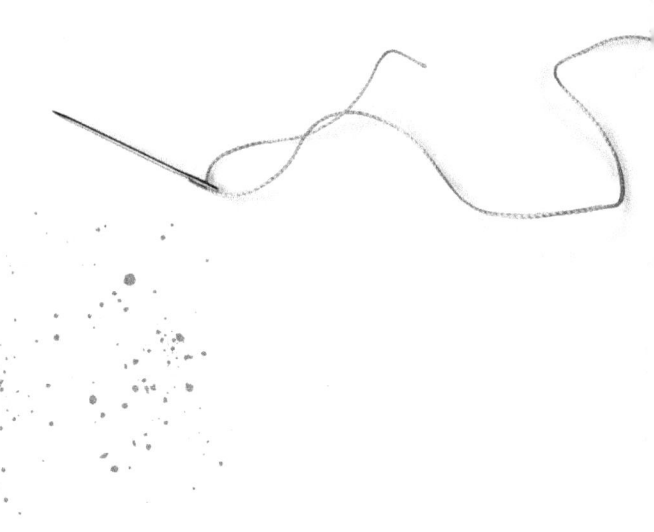

I am done
carrying your
burdens,
fixing your
problems,
holding your
shame,
forgiving your
sin,
taking your
blame.

I am done being the one crucified on your cross.

I love you.
~~I do.~~
~~I do.~~
~~I do.~~

I did.

My ___*story*___ & me

Loving you was my *greatest* mistake.

I never understood the 'good' in goodbye.

until you.

I hate
that you
took away
the parts of *me*
you fell in love with.

In your freedom,
I was still shackled to you.

Do I miss *him*?
or the *attention*?

I filled your absence with similar men,
hoping to rewrite the story's end.

Here I go again,
mistaking familiarity for ~~love~~ _____.

Love.
a mixtape
labeled
maybe, ours.

The moment I said
"hello,"
I wanted
you to be
my last
"goodbye."

Nothing is more *addicting*
than unrequited love.
the *hope* of
being wanted back
is *intoxicating*.

My ___*story*___ & me

I fell in love with a story that was not ours.

165

He lingered there,
suspended in time,
savored the moment
& created a memory
of *me.*

the delusions of my mind.

Everything I have
is not what I needed,
but what I wanted.

you included.

You were never *mine,*
but it didn't make
what I felt
any less
real.

I longed for you from the moment our eyes met,
even when yours didn't search for *mine*.

My affection remains,
unseen & unreturned.

Destination,
you.
departure,
you.

Falling for you felt as easy as breathing,
yet as painful as losing air.

Play.
pause.
stop.
rewind.
the story of
you & I.

The one thing
I hated about myself
he loved the most
he said
it made me
real
it made me
human.

I was imperfectly his.

My ___*story*___ & me

"*It's not you, it's me,*"
still impacts our
"*we*".

I am still standing where your absence left me, heartbroken.

You were
always
the intermission
in my life.

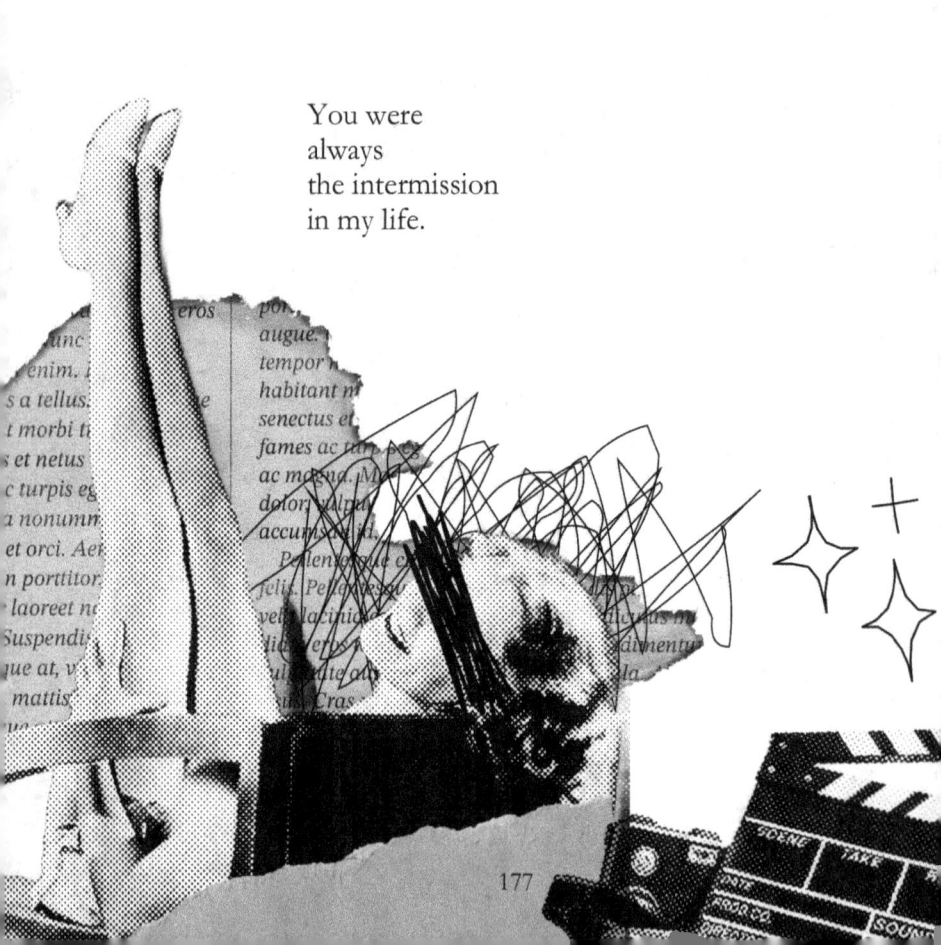

You asked me once
if I could settle for less.
to be honest,
no.
I will always want more,
but I can choose less.
less means there is hope for more;
it's not *gone.*

maybe then, you'd be mine.

You linger in the echoes of what might have been.

You were my dream,
until reality stole you away.

I have
patches
on my heart,
written
with all our
memories _____.

Us
a slow extinguishing
of a flame,
desperate to stay
alight.

My ~~story~~ & me

You said,
I was your
sunset
in the
storm.

you never waited to see the skies clear.

If you mean forever,
you'll always try;
but if not,
never say forever,
because forever
makes me cry.

My ___story___ & me

Forever _____,
a word you forgot.

How do you keep from breaking someone's heart?
it's a delicate dance,
one wrong step—
everything can tumble to pieces.
no clear-cut instructions,
no tried-and-true map
leading to a happy ending.
the path is filled with
emotional pitfalls & minefields,
ready to detonate at any moment.

no.

it doesn't matter
how you start—
it's already *the end.*

It's a moment
of heart-wrenching desperation—
wanting someone so badly,
knowing the credits are playing.

To think
we were
happy
not long ago.
now I am
running
from the
inevitable.

the breakup.

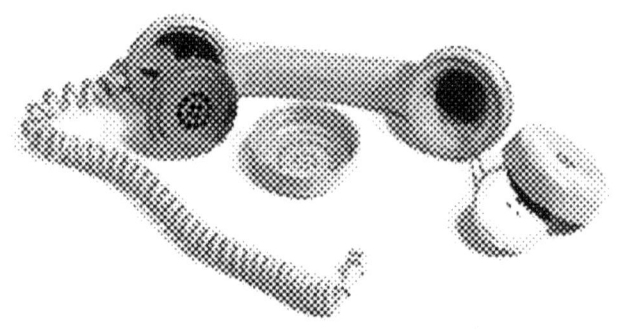

One phone call,
dial tone.
two hearts,
one broken.
disconnected.

Everything we had shared was over in ten seconds.

Sometimes,
even the most
beautiful love stories,
have an
expiration date.

Our souls were intertwined,
you & I.
tangled forever,
never to be unraveled.

even with the cracks, you filled the spaces.

My ___*story*___ & me

You were kind when you broke my heart,
& it only made me love you *more*.

I wish I'd loved you then,
as much as I miss you now.

~~Heartbreak~~ _____
consumes every inch of you,
leaving no room for the appetite
that once fed your joy.

I would've
savored
in us
a little longer
before
we became
~~strangers~~ _____.

The worst thing wasn't losing you,
but losing the light you gave my days.

You were always
the *right* person,
there was never
a wrong time.

just *choices*.

Suffocating
in an
unending loop
of memories,
examining every
detail
to trace the
breadcrumbs
that led to
the bitter end.
a tortuous cycle,
each fleeting moment
of relief
replaced by a
haunting reminder
of what once *was*.

reminders of ~~us~~ _____.
reminders of ~~you~~ _____.

Do thoughts of me cross your mind,
or am I condemned to be
the fading reflection
of a once familiar lover?

I still hold onto
the fragments of us:
stolen glances,
whispered promises,
shared dreams
that were
cruelly interrupted.

Remember?
remember?
remember?
remember?
~~no.~~
yes.

the battlefield of my heart.

My _story_ & me

Erasing you,
erases me,
& everything
that made us
"we."

I hate knowing
you're out there,
living your life
without me.

You were
the evidence
that real love
existed.

will I find it again?

I still hold your secrets,
after all this time.

do you still hold mine?

My ~~story~~ & me

If love is free
then why did it cost me
~~everything~~ _____ ?

It's incredible how a person can make you feel small, insecure, & vulnerable all over again.

my past & me.

One day,
you will love me
the way
I loved you.
one day,
you'll think of me
the way
I thought of you.
one day,
you'll cry for me
the way
I cried for you.
one day,
you'll want me
&
I won't want _you_.

My *teachers*
& me

My <u>*story*</u> & me

People always
filled in the ~~blanks~~ _____
of who I was.

handwritten in invisible ink.

Grow beyond their expectations,
when you can't fit into their mold.

People may never
understand
the amount of
time
courage
&
effort
it took to say
no.

~~Courage~~ _____,
is to step
into something
with
~~fear~~ _____,
it's not
the same
as
~~fearless~~ _____,

it's *greater.*
it's *braver.*

216

My ___*story*___ & me

It's never selfish
to take care of yourself
even when people
tell you otherwise

a declaration of self-love & worth.

I don't need your *permission*
to earn *respect.*
I don't need your *acceptance*
to be *who I am.*
I don't need your *approval*
to know *what I want.*
I don't need your *time*
to fill *mine.*
I don't need your *support*
to stand *tall.*
I don't need your *recognition*
to be *successful.*
I don't need your *opinions*
to make *choices.*
I don't need your *love*
to love *myself.*

I just need me.
I always did.

courage

My ___*story*___ & me

Your choices are yours.

always have been.

I chose my peace
over your approval.
I walked away
& let you go.

the day my life began.

My house looks different;
it breathes life,
vibrant and proud.
no more trespassers,
no more allowed.

I built my fences.

I am *art*.
my existence
is a masterpiece.

My ___*story*___ & me

~~Relationships~~ _____,
are fingerprints
on our souls.
reminders,
of everything we
do,
did,
don't,
have.

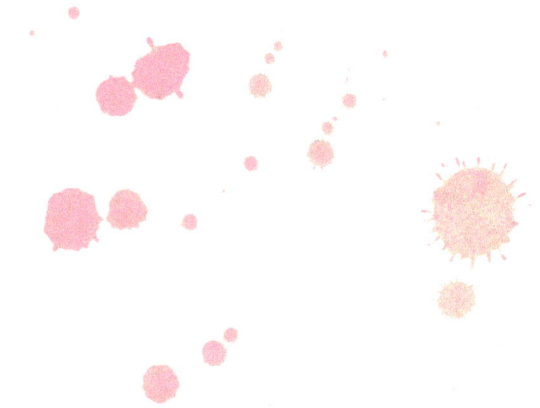

A thousand hellos,
too many goodbyes.
people disappear
without even knowing
why.

Cherish the people
who let you live life freely,
holding no expectations
beyond the love
you share for each other.

The greatest challenge
lies in
etching into
memory
those fleeting *moments*
we yearn to hold onto
forever.

Hurting people
hurt,
loving people
who *love* people.

it was never your fault.

It's the little things that say a lot about a person.
the big things are just a distraction.

consistency versus exceptionalism.

Little acts of kindness,
unappreciated in their presence,
become *could've, would've, should've*
moments in your absence.

you are a gift.

Call it quits
when wasted time
is on someone
who makes you
only an option,
never a priority.

choose yourself.

Never say
you *will*
if you
don't plan to
start.

Promises are seeds;
only sow them if you're ready to watch them grow.

The girl told the boy,
"I have a heart that's too big
to receive a love that's too little."

know your worth.

~~Doubt~~ _____,
once allowed to
linger,
becomes a
thief
of dreams,
a silent
assassin
of potential.

turn the 'what if' into 'what now'.

The mother
told the daughter,
"true confidence
dwells in
authenticity,
embracing flaws
without apology."

The girl learned
to let *reason*
be her anchor,
understanding
her compass,
courage
her shield,
& *love*
her driving force.

I refuse to live a stationary life.

A broken heart
still beats.
within its pain,
hope
quietly sleeps.

Hope in today for peace in tomorrow.

"*I'm okay,*"
"*I'm fine,*"
don't tell people
how you are,
they tell people
what your not.

what you feel,
how you feel,
matters.

Even in the darkness,
   your embers still
      glow.

The old woman told
the little girl,
"hold the lessons
of bad memories;
they are the canvas
where you paint
the masterpiece of
good ones."

When I think back
on my younger self,
all I want to do is
hold her,
carry her tears,
remind her
that I'll always
protect her.

she was always enough.

My _story_ & me

My heart
grieved for the
girl
who hated
what she became
& couldn't love
who she always
was.

embrace your past & present self with unwavering grace.

243

The older self
told the younger self,
"setbacks are a pause;
not a stop in life."

I am not in denial.
I am *lost*
in rebellious *hope*.

An optimistic
pessimist,
searching for
promise
in a world of
~~uncertainty~~ _____.

It brings me peace
that parts of me
will forever be printed
in memory,
on paper & ink.

Forgiveness.
acceptance.
love.
grace.

things that cost nothing to *give*,
but mean everything to *receive*.

my teachers & me.

I saved me
from
myself.

my greatest achievement.

ROSEWOOD

Acknowledgements

To all my readers, thank you so much for taking the time to dive into my thoughts. I hope you find pieces of your own story & emotions in my words, recognizing the beautiful complexity of our human experiences and the worth of every feeling we navigate. Just like art, life is full of messy imperfections, but it's those imperfections that make it uniquely beautiful.

To my Heavenly Father, thank you for creating me with such care & purpose. My mind and experiences are gifts that have shaped me, allowing me to bring positive change and be a source of comfort for others. I am forever grateful for your guidance and the talents you've given me to leave a meaningful mark on this world.

To my husband, you are everything I could have ever wanted. You inspire me & remind me daily of unconditional love through your words & actions. Thank you for constantly challenging me to be the best version of myself, & for giving me the courage & motivation to share my words with the world. *You are my gravity, keeping me grounded.* I love you today, tomorrow, forever.

To my parents, thank you for your endless love and for nurturing my passion for art and writing. You've always been my biggest supporters, present at every milestone in my life. Your unwavering encouragement has shaped who I am today, & I see so much of myself in you, which I celebrate every day.

To Joseph Adam, this vision would not be possible without your incredibly talented mind. Your art captures & evokes a spectrum of emotions that remind us of our humanity, illustrating how beautiful it is to embrace *vulnerability & bravery* in a world that often seeks to paint us in black and white. Thank you for your constant support, love, & encouragement. I eagerly anticipate many more collaborations & projects together in the future.

To Skarlet, my dark angel who has dedicated so much time & energy to this project to support me: thank you for your candor & encouraging words that helped bring my vision to life. Since I met you, you've been a steadfast advocate for my voice, & I'm honored to call you my friend. Your endless voice notes on tough days kept me inspired & motivated when I felt tired or frustrated. I appreciate you immensely. Love you BIG.

To my BETA & ARC readers, your feedback & enthusiasm have given me the courage to share my art with the world. I deeply appreciate your dedication & constant encouragement—my dancing spirit thrives on your support. Thank you!

To Tisa, you truly know & understand my heart, my kindred spirit. Your love & passion for writing touch me deeply. You've inspired me to keep writing & demonstrated the power of consistency & dedication. I cherish our late-night poetry sessions & our talks about life's complexities. You are my sparkle in my pink heart. I'm keeping you forever. I love you dearly!

To Ana, thank you for always being a listening ear and for taking such a genuine interest in everything I love. Your support in all my passions & hobbies means the world to me. Your friendship is truly special!

To the Booksta community & followers, I wanted to take a moment to express my heartfelt appreciation for the incredible friendship, love, & support y'all have shown me. Your enthusiasm for books & cultivating genuine connections have made my journey as a writer life changing. I adore each and every one of you!

To everyone who has come and gone from my life, thank you for being part of my story. Your presence, with all its joys and challenges, was a catalyst for allowing my words to be on paper. I appreciate the beautiful and tough lessons—it made me stronger! It made me a *badass.*

About the Author

Kate Rosewood is an OC girl who adores all things pink & can often be found lost in books or crafting heartfelt poetry. When she's not writing, she's likely indulging in In-N-Out Burger or exploring the outdoors with her husband.

In her debut poetry volume, "My ~~story~~ & me," Kate Rosewood delves into the complexities of being human through mind, body, & spirit. Her collection explores themes of mental health, relationships, acceptance, healing, & growth. Kate's poetry is characterized by brevity, simplicity, & lyrical quality, fostering a direct & relatable connection with readers. By integrating art as an essential element, she enhances storytelling to evoke deep emotions from readers. Her aspiration is for her poetry to speak when others cannot, helping individuals find their own voices through her words.

 www.instagram.com/katerosewoodpoetry

 www.katerosewood.com